This Journal Belongs to

_____

Want some free content?
Sign up at
23streams.com/bonus
Your code: 9j&37C

Follow on:
Youtube

Facebook
Instagram
Tiktok

Please Leave A Review On Amazon
And
Order Your Journal For Psalms 51-100

Shop our other books at 23streams.com

© 23streams. All rights reserved. No part of this publication may be reproduced, distributed, or transmitted, in any form or by any means, including photocopying, recording, or other electronic or mechanical methods, without prior written permission of the publisher, except in the case of brief quotations embodied in critical reviews and certain other noncommercial uses permitted by copyright law.

THE BOOK OF PSALMS 1-50 JOURNAL FOR WOMEN
Chapter a Day Listening Prayer with Gratitude Journal

This Daily Gratitude & Listening Prayer Journal can be used in combination with other 23streams.com resources or independently.

We have provided Guided Listening Prayer videos for each of these psalms on our website.

To access the website and choose the Psalm you would like to meditate on use your smartphone camera and point it at the QR code in the top right corner of the Psalm page.

If you do not have access to a QR code reader you can go to: 23streams.com/qr/psalm-1-50-journal-women

All verses in this journal are from the WEB translation which is in the Public Domain.

Date _____

Psalm 1:3

Use QR code to access the listening prayer videos

> HE WILL BE LIKE A TREE PLANTED BY THE STREAMS OF WATER, THAT PRODUCES ITS FRUIT IN ITS SEASON, WHOSE LEAF ALSO DOES NOT WITHER. WHATEVER HE DOES SHALL PROSPER.

Daily Gratitude

I am grateful for...

1 _____
2 _____
3 _____

Today would be great if...

1 _____
2 _____

What affirmations does God have for you today?

1 _____
2 _____

Who would you like to pray for and bless today?

1 _____
2 _____

Listening Prayer

Read or listen to the scripture, follow the prompts in silence for 1-2 min.

First Reading

Listen and feel the word of God over you. Take notes on what you felt as the word of God washed over you.

_____
_____
_____
_____
_____
_____

Second Reading

Bring awareness and mindfulness to anything the Lord is pointing out and offer them to God. Take notes on anything that is highlighted.

_____
_____
_____
_____
_____
_____

Third Reading

Ask God about the highlighted things. Do you feel called to do anything? Listen to God and take notes on anything you hear.

_____
_____
_____
_____
_____
_____

Date _____

Psalm 2
2:7-9

Use QR code to access the listening prayer videos

YAHWEH SAID TO ME, "YOU ARE MY SON. TODAY I HAVE BECOME YOUR FATHER. ASK OF ME, AND I WILL GIVE THE NATIONS FOR YOUR INHERITANCE, THE UTTERMOST PARTS OF THE EARTH FOR YOUR POSSESSION. YOU SHALL BREAK THEM WITH A ROD OF IRON. YOU SHALL DASH THEM IN PIECES LIKE A POTTER'S VESSEL."

Daily Gratitude

I am grateful for...

1 _____

2 _____

3 _____

Today would be great if...

1 _____

2 _____

What affirmations does God have for you today?

1 _____

2 _____

Who would you like to pray for and bless today?

1 _____

2 _____

Listening Prayer

Read or listen to the scripture, follow the prompts in silence for 1-2 min.

First Reading

Listen and feel the word of God over you. Take notes on what you felt as the word of God washed over you.

_____
_____
_____
_____
_____
_____

Second Reading

Bring awareness and mindfulness to anything the Lord is pointing out and offer them to God. Take notes on anything that is highlighted.

_____
_____
_____
_____
_____
_____

Third Reading

Ask God about the highlighted things. Do you feel called to do anything? Listen to God and take notes on anything you hear.

_____
_____
_____
_____
_____
_____

Date _____

Psalm 3
3:2-4

Use QR code to access the listening prayer videos

MANY THERE ARE WHO SAY OF MY SOUL, "THERE IS NO HELP FOR HIM IN GOD." SELAH. BUT YOU, YAHWEH, ARE A SHIELD AROUND ME, MY GLORY, AND THE ONE WHO LIFTS UP MY HEAD. I CRY TO YAHWEH WITH MY VOICE, AND HE ANSWERS ME OUT OF HIS HOLY HILL. SELAH.

Daily Gratitude

I am grateful for...

1 _____

2 _____

3 _____

Today would be great if...

1 _____

2 _____

What affirmations does God have for you today?

1 _____

2 _____

Who would you like to pray for and bless today?

1 _____

2 _____

Listening Prayer

Read or listen to the scripture, follow the prompts in silence for 1-2 min.

First Reading

Listen and feel the word of God over you. Take notes on what you felt as the word of God washed over you.

_____
_____
_____
_____
_____
_____

Second Reading

Bring awareness and mindfulness to anything the Lord is pointing out and offer them to God. Take notes on anything that is highlighted.

_____
_____
_____
_____
_____
_____

Third Reading

Ask God about the highlighted things. Do you feel called to do anything? Listen to God and take notes on anything you hear.

_____
_____
_____
_____
_____
_____

Date _____

Psalm 4
4:6-8

Use QR code to access the listening prayer videos

YAHWEH, LET THE LIGHT OF YOUR FACE SHINE ON US. YOU HAVE PUT GLADNESS IN MY HEART, MORE THAN WHEN THEIR GRAIN AND THEIR NEW WINE ARE INCREASED. IN PEACE I WILL BOTH LAY MYSELF DOWN AND SLEEP, FOR YOU, YAHWEH ALONE, MAKE ME LIVE IN SAFETY.

Daily Gratitude

I am grateful for...

1 _____
2 _____
3 _____

Today would be great if...

1 _____
2 _____

What affirmations does God have for you today?

1 _____
2 _____

Who would you like to pray for and bless today?

1 _____
2 _____

Listening Prayer

Read or listen to the scripture, follow the prompts in silence for 1-2 min.

First Reading

Listen and feel the word of God over you. Take notes on what you felt as the word of God washed over you.

_____
_____
_____
_____
_____
_____

Second Reading

Bring awareness and mindfulness to anything the Lord is pointing out and offer them to God. Take notes on anything that is highlighted.

_____
_____
_____
_____
_____
_____

Third Reading

Ask God about the highlighted things. Do you feel called to do anything? Listen to God and take notes on anything you hear.

_____
_____
_____
_____
_____
_____

Date

Psalm 5
5:11-12

Use QR code to access the listening prayer videos

BUT LET ALL THOSE WHO TAKE REFUGE IN YOU REJOICE. LET THEM ALWAYS SHOUT FOR JOY, BECAUSE YOU DEFEND THEM. LET THEM ALSO WHO LOVE YOUR NAME BE JOYFUL IN YOU. FOR YOU WILL BLESS THE RIGHTEOUS. YAHWEH, YOU WILL SURROUND HIM WITH FAVOR AS WITH A SHIELD.

Daily Gratitude

I am grateful for...

1
2
3

Today would be great if...

1
2

What affirmations does God have for you today?

1
2

Who would you like to pray for and bless today?

1
2

Listening Prayer

Read or listen to the scripture, follow the prompts in silence for 1-2 min.

First Reading

Listen and feel the word of God over you. Take notes on what you felt as the word of God washed over you.

_____
_____
_____
_____
_____

Second Reading

Bring awareness and mindfulness to anything the Lord is pointing out and offer them to God. Take notes on anything that is highlighted.

_____
_____
_____
_____
_____

Third Reading

Ask God about the highlighted things. Do you feel called to do anything? Listen to God and take notes on anything you hear.

_____
_____
_____
_____
_____

Date: _____

Psalm 6
6:9-10

Use QR code to access the listening prayer videos

YAHWEH HAS HEARD MY SUPPLICATION. YAHWEH ACCEPTS MY PRAYER. MAY ALL MY ENEMIES BE ASHAMED AND DISMAYED. THEY SHALL TURN BACK, THEY SHALL BE DISGRACED SUDDENLY.

Daily Gratitude

I am grateful for...

1 _____

2 _____

3 _____

Today would be great if...

1 _____

2 _____

What affirmations does God have for you today?

1 _____

2 _____

Who would you like to pray for and bless today?

1 _____

2 _____

Listening Prayer

Read or listen to the scripture, follow the prompts in silence for 1-2 min.

First Reading

Listen and feel the word of God over you. Take notes on what you felt as the word of God washed over you.

_____
_____
_____
_____
_____
_____

Second Reading

Bring awareness and mindfulness to anything the Lord is pointing out and offer them to God. Take notes on anything that is highlighted.

_____
_____
_____
_____
_____
_____

Third Reading

Ask God about the highlighted things. Do you feel called to do anything? Listen to God and take notes on anything you hear.

_____
_____
_____
_____
_____
_____

Date _____

Psalm 7
7:10-11

Use QR code to access the listening prayer videos

> MY SHIELD IS WITH GOD, WHO SAVES THE UPRIGHT IN HEART. GOD IS A RIGHTEOUS JUDGE, YES, A GOD WHO HAS INDIGNATION EVERY DAY.

Daily Gratitude

I am grateful for...

1 _____

2 _____

3 _____

Today would be great if...

1 _____

2 _____

What affirmations does God have for you today?

1 _____

2 _____

Who would you like to pray for and bless today?

1 _____

2 _____

Listening Prayer

Read or listen to the scripture, follow the prompts in silence for 1-2 min.

First Reading

Listen and feel the word of God over you. Take notes on what you felt as the word of God washed over you.

_____
_____
_____
_____
_____

Second Reading

Bring awareness and mindfulness to anything the Lord is pointing out and offer them to God. Take notes on anything that is highlighted.

_____
_____
_____
_____
_____

Third Reading

Ask God about the highlighted things. Do you feel called to do anything? Listen to God and take notes on anything you hear.

_____
_____
_____
_____
_____

Date
Psalm 8
8:3-5

Use QR code to access the listening prayer videos

WHEN I CONSIDER YOUR HEAVENS, THE WORK OF YOUR FINGERS, THE MOON AND THE STARS WHICH YOU HAVE ORDAINED; WHAT IS MAN, THAT YOU THINK OF HIM? WHAT IS THE SON OF MAN, THAT YOU CARE FOR HIM? FOR YOU HAVE MADE HIM A LITTLE LOWER THAN THE ANGELS, AND CROWNED HIM WITH GLORY AND HONOR.

Daily Gratitude

I am grateful for...

1
2
3

Today would be great if...

1
2

What affirmations does God have for you today?

1
2

Who would you like to pray for and bless today?

1
2

Listening Prayer

Read or listen to the scripture, follow the prompts in silence for 1-2 min.

First Reading

Listen and feel the word of God over you. Take notes on what you felt as the word of God washed over you.

_____
_____
_____
_____
_____
_____

Second Reading

Bring awareness and mindfulness to anything the Lord is pointing out and offer them to God. Take notes on anything that is highlighted.

_____
_____
_____
_____
_____
_____

Third Reading

Ask God about the highlighted things. Do you feel called to do anything? Listen to God and take notes on anything you hear.

_____
_____
_____
_____
_____
_____

Date _____

Psalm 9
9:18-20

Use QR code to access the listening prayer videos

For the needy shall not always be forgotten, nor the hope of the poor perish forever. Arise, Yahweh! Don't let man prevail. Let the nations be judged in your sight. Put them in fear, Yahweh. Let the nations know that they are only men. Selah.

Daily Gratitude

I am grateful for...

1 _____

2 _____

3 _____

Today would be great if...

1 _____

2 _____

What affirmations does God have for you today?

1 _____

2 _____

Who would you like to pray for and bless today?

1 _____

2 _____

Listening Prayer

Read or listen to the scripture, follow the prompts in silence for 1-2 min.

First Reading

Listen and feel the word of God over you. Take notes on what you felt as the word of God washed over you.

Second Reading

Bring awareness and mindfulness to anything the Lord is pointing out and offer them to God. Take notes on anything that is highlighted.

Third Reading

Ask God about the highlighted things. Do you feel called to do anything? Listen to God and take notes on anything you hear.

Date

Psalm 10
10:17-18

Use QR code to access the listening prayer videos

YAHWEH, YOU HAVE HEARD THE DESIRE OF THE HUMBLE. YOU WILL PREPARE THEIR HEART. YOU WILL CAUSE YOUR EAR TO HEAR, TO JUDGE THE FATHERLESS AND THE OPPRESSED, THAT MAN WHO IS OF THE EARTH MAY TERRIFY NO MORE.

Daily Gratitude

I am grateful for...

1
2
3

Today would be great if...

1
2

What affirmations does God have for you today?

1
2

Who would you like to pray for and bless today?

1
2

Listening Prayer

Read or listen to the scripture, follow the prompts in silence for 1-2 min.

First Reading

Listen and feel the word of God over you. Take notes on what you felt as the word of God washed over you.

_____
_____
_____
_____
_____
_____

Second Reading

Bring awareness and mindfulness to anything the Lord is pointing out and offer them to God. Take notes on anything that is highlighted.

_____
_____
_____
_____
_____
_____

Third Reading

Ask God about the highlighted things. Do you feel called to do anything? Listen to God and take notes on anything you hear.

_____
_____
_____
_____
_____
_____

Date _____

Psalm 11
11:4-5

Use QR code to access the listening prayer videos

YAHWEH IS IN HIS HOLY TEMPLE. YAHWEH IS ON HIS THRONE IN HEAVEN. HIS EYES OBSERVE. HIS EYES EXAMINE THE CHILDREN OF MEN. YAHWEH EXAMINES THE RIGHTEOUS, BUT HIS SOUL HATES THE WICKED AND HIM WHO LOVES VIOLENCE.

Daily Gratitude

I am grateful for...

1 _____

2 _____

3 _____

Today would be great if...

1 _____

2 _____

What affirmations does God have for you today?

1 _____

2 _____

Who would you like to pray for and bless today?

1 _____

2 _____

Listening Prayer

Read or listen to the scripture, follow the prompts in silence for 1-2 min.

First Reading

Listen and feel the word of God over you. Take notes on what you felt as the word of God washed over you.

Second Reading

Bring awareness and mindfulness to anything the Lord is pointing out and offer them to God. Take notes on anything that is highlighted.

Third Reading

Ask God about the highlighted things. Do you feel called to do anything? Listen to God and take notes on anything you hear.

Date _____

Psalm 12
12:5-6

Use QR code to access the listening prayer videos

"Because of the oppression of the weak and because of the groaning of the needy, I will now arise," says Yahweh; "I will set him in safety from those who malign him." Yahweh's words are flawless words, as silver refined in a clay furnace, purified seven times.

Daily Gratitude

I am grateful for...

1 _____

2 _____

3 _____

Today would be great if...

1 _____

2 _____

What affirmations does God have for you today?

1 _____

2 _____

Who would you like to pray for and bless today?

1 _____

2 _____

Listening Prayer

Read or listen to the scripture, follow the prompts in silence for 1-2 min.

First Reading

Listen and feel the word of God over you. Take notes on what you felt as the word of God washed over you.

Second Reading

Bring awareness and mindfulness to anything the Lord is pointing out and offer them to God. Take notes on anything that is highlighted.

Third Reading

Ask God about the highlighted things. Do you feel called to do anything? Listen to God and take notes on anything you hear.

Date

Psalm 13
13:1-2 & 5-6

Use QR code to access the listening prayer videos

How long, Yahweh? Will you forget me forever? How long will you hide your face from me? How long shall I take counsel in my soul, having sorrow in my heart every day? How long shall my enemy triumph over me?... But I trust in your loving kindness. My heart rejoices in your salvation. I will sing to Yahweh, because he has been good to me.

Daily Gratitude

I am grateful for...

1
2
3

Today would be great if...

1
2

What affirmations does God have for you today?

1
2

Who would you like to pray for and bless today?

1
2

Listening Prayer

Read or listen to the scripture, follow the prompts in silence for 1-2 min.

First Reading

Listen and feel the word of God over you. Take notes on what you felt as the word of God washed over you.

Second Reading

Bring awareness and mindfulness to anything the Lord is pointing out and offer them to God. Take notes on anything that is highlighted.

Third Reading

Ask God about the highlighted things. Do you feel called to do anything? Listen to God and take notes on anything you hear.

Date _____

Psalm 14
14:1-3

Use QR code to access the listening prayer videos

The fool has said in his heart, "There is no God." They are corrupt. They have done abominable deeds. There is no one who does good. Yahweh looked down from heaven on the children of men, to see if there were any who understood, who sought after God. They have all gone aside. They have together become corrupt. There is no one who does good, no, not one.

Daily Gratitude

I am grateful for...

1 _____

2 _____

3 _____

Today would be great if...

1 _____

2 _____

What affirmations does God have for you today?

1 _____

2 _____

Who would you like to pray for and bless today?

1 _____

2 _____

Listening Prayer

Read or listen to the scripture, follow the prompts in silence for 1-2 min.

First Reading

Listen and feel the word of God over you. Take notes on what you felt as the word of God washed over you.

Second Reading

Bring awareness and mindfulness to anything the Lord is pointing out and offer them to God. Take notes on anything that is highlighted.

Third Reading

Ask God about the highlighted things. Do you feel called to do anything? Listen to God and take notes on anything you hear.

Date _____

Psalm 15
15:1-3

Use QR code to access the listening prayer videos

YAHWEH, WHO SHALL DWELL IN YOUR SANCTUARY? WHO SHALL LIVE ON YOUR HOLY HILL? HE WHO WALKS BLAMELESSLY AND DOES WHAT IS RIGHT, AND SPEAKS TRUTH IN HIS HEART; HE WHO DOESN'T SLANDER WITH HIS TONGUE, NOR DOES EVIL TO HIS FRIEND, NOR CASTS SLURS AGAINST HIS FELLOW MAN;

Daily Gratitude

I am grateful for...

1 _____
2 _____
3 _____

Today would be great if...

1 _____
2 _____

What affirmations does God have for you today?

1 _____
2 _____

Who would you like to pray for and bless today?

1 _____
2 _____

Listening Prayer

Read or listen to the scripture, follow the prompts in silence for 1-2 min.

First Reading

Listen and feel the word of God over you. Take notes on what you felt as the word of God washed over you.

Second Reading

Bring awareness and mindfulness to anything the Lord is pointing out and offer them to God. Take notes on anything that is highlighted.

Third Reading

Ask God about the highlighted things. Do you feel called to do anything? Listen to God and take notes on anything you hear.

Date _____

Psalm 16
16:8-11

Use QR code to access the listening prayer videos

I HAVE SET YAHWEH ALWAYS BEFORE ME. BECAUSE HE IS AT MY RIGHT HAND, I SHALL NOT BE MOVED. THEREFORE MY HEART IS GLAD, AND MY TONGUE REJOICES. MY BODY SHALL ALSO DWELL IN SAFETY. FOR YOU WILL NOT LEAVE MY SOUL IN SHEOL, NEITHER WILL YOU ALLOW YOUR HOLY ONE TO SEE CORRUPTION. YOU WILL SHOW ME THE PATH OF LIFE. IN YOUR PRESENCE IS FULLNESS OF JOY. IN YOUR RIGHT HAND THERE ARE PLEASURES FOREVER MORE.

Daily Gratitude

I am grateful for...

1 _____
2 _____
3 _____

Today would be great if...

1 _____
2 _____

What affirmations does God have for you today?

1 _____
2 _____

Who would you like to pray for and bless today?

1 _____
2 _____

Listening Prayer

Read or listen to the scripture, follow the prompts in silence for 1-2 min.

First Reading

Listen and feel the word of God over you. Take notes on what you felt as the word of God washed over you.

_____
_____
_____
_____
_____
_____

Second Reading

Bring awareness and mindfulness to anything the Lord is pointing out and offer them to God. Take notes on anything that is highlighted.

_____
_____
_____
_____
_____
_____

Third Reading

Ask God about the highlighted things. Do you feel called to do anything? Listen to God and take notes on anything you hear.

_____
_____
_____
_____
_____
_____

Date _____

Psalm 17
17:5-8

Use QR code to access the listening prayer videos

My steps have held fast to your paths. My feet have not slipped. I have called on you, for you will answer me, God. Turn your ear to me. Hear my speech. Show your marvelous loving kindness, you who save those who take refuge by your right hand from their enemies. Keep me as the apple of your eye. Hide me under the shadow of your wings,

Daily Gratitude

I am grateful for...

1 _____

2 _____

3 _____

Today would be great if...

1 _____

2 _____

What affirmations does God have for you today?

1 _____

2 _____

Who would you like to pray for and bless today?

1 _____

2 _____

Listening Prayer

Read or listen to the scripture, follow the prompts in silence for 1-2 min.

First Reading

Listen and feel the word of God over you. Take notes on what you felt as the word of God washed over you.

Second Reading

Bring awareness and mindfulness to anything the Lord is pointing out and offer them to God. Take notes on anything that is highlighted.

Third Reading

Ask God about the highlighted things. Do you feel called to do anything? Listen to God and take notes on anything you hear.

Date _____

Psalm 18
18:46-49

Use QR code to access the listening prayer videos

Yahweh lives! Blessed be my rock. Exalted be the God of my salvation, even the God who executes vengeance for me, and subdues peoples under me. He rescues me from my enemies. Yes, you lift me up above those who rise up against me. You deliver me from the violent man. Therefore I will give thanks to you, Yahweh, among the nations, and will sing praises to your name.

Daily Gratitude

I am grateful for...

1 _____

2 _____

3 _____

Today would be great if...

1 _____

2 _____

What affirmations does God have for you today?

1 _____

2 _____

Who would you like to pray for and bless today?

1 _____

2 _____

Listening Prayer

Read or listen to the scripture, follow the prompts in silence for 1-2 min.

First Reading

Listen and feel the word of God over you. Take notes on what you felt as the word of God washed over you.

_____
_____
_____
_____
_____
_____

Second Reading

Bring awareness and mindfulness to anything the Lord is pointing out and offer them to God. Take notes on anything that is highlighted.

_____
_____
_____
_____
_____
_____

Third Reading

Ask God about the highlighted things. Do you feel called to do anything? Listen to God and take notes on anything you hear.

_____
_____
_____
_____
_____
_____

Date _____

Psalm 19
19:13-14

Use QR code to access the listening prayer videos

Keep back your servant also from presumptuous sins. Let them not have dominion over me. Then I will be upright. I will be blameless and innocent of great transgression. Let the words of my mouth and the meditation of my heart be acceptable in your sight, Yahweh, my rock, and my redeemer.

Daily Gratitude

I am grateful for...

1 _____

2 _____

3 _____

Today would be great if...

1 _____

2 _____

What affirmations does God have for you today?

1 _____

2 _____

Who would you like to pray for and bless today?

1 _____

2 _____

Listening Prayer

Read or listen to the scripture, follow the prompts in silence for 1-2 min.

First Reading

Listen and feel the word of God over you. Take notes on what you felt as the word of God washed over you.

_____
_____
_____
_____
_____
_____

Second Reading

Bring awareness and mindfulness to anything the Lord is pointing out and offer them to God. Take notes on anything that is highlighted.

_____
_____
_____
_____
_____
_____

Third Reading

Ask God about the highlighted things. Do you feel called to do anything? Listen to God and take notes on anything you hear.

_____
_____
_____
_____
_____
_____

Date

Psalm 20
20:1-5

Use QR code to access the listening prayer videos

May Yahweh answer you in the day of trouble. May the name of the God of Jacob set you up on high, send you help from the sanctuary, grant you support from Zion, remember all your offerings, and accept your burned sacrifice. Selah. May he grant you your heart's desire, and fulfill all your counsel. We will triumph in your salvation. In the name of our God, we will set up our banners.

Daily Gratitude

I am grateful for...

1
2
3

Today would be great if...

1
2

What affirmations does God have for you today?

1
2

Who would you like to pray for and bless today?

1
2

Listening Prayer

Read or listen to the scripture, follow the prompts in silence for 1-2 min.

First Reading

Listen and feel the word of God over you. Take notes on what you felt as the word of God washed over you.

___

Second Reading

Bring awareness and mindfulness to anything the Lord is pointing out and offer them to God. Take notes on anything that is highlighted.

___

Third Reading

Ask God about the highlighted things. Do you feel called to do anything? Listen to God and take notes on anything you hear.

Date

Psalm 21
21:1-3

Use QR code to access the listening prayer videos

THE KING REJOICES IN YOUR STRENGTH, YAHWEH! HOW GREATLY HE REJOICES IN YOUR SALVATION! YOU HAVE GIVEN HIM HIS HEART'S DESIRE, AND HAVE NOT WITHHELD THE REQUEST OF HIS LIPS. SELAH. FOR YOU MEET HIM WITH THE BLESSINGS OF GOODNESS. YOU SET A CROWN OF FINE GOLD ON HIS HEAD.

Daily Gratitude

I am grateful for...

1
2
3

Today would be great if...

1
2

What affirmations does God have for you today?

1
2

Who would you like to pray for and bless today?

1
2

Listening Prayer

Read or listen to the scripture, follow the prompts in silence for 1-2 min.

First Reading

Listen and feel the word of God over you. Take notes on what you felt as the word of God washed over you.

_____
_____
_____
_____
_____

Second Reading

Bring awareness and mindfulness to anything the Lord is pointing out and offer them to God. Take notes on anything that is highlighted.

_____
_____
_____
_____
_____

Third Reading

Ask God about the highlighted things. Do you feel called to do anything? Listen to God and take notes on anything you hear.

_____
_____
_____
_____
_____

Date

Psalm 22
22:2-4

My God, I cry in the daytime, but you don't answer; in the night season, and am not silent. But you are holy you who inhabit the praises of Israel. Our fathers trusted in you. They trusted, and you delivered them.

Daily Gratitude

I am grateful for...

1 _____

2 _____

3 _____

Today would be great if...

1 _____

2 _____

What affirmations does God have for you today?

1 _____

2 _____

Who would you like to pray for and bless today?

1 _____

2 _____

Listening Prayer

Read or listen to the scripture, follow the prompts in silence for 1-2 min.

First Reading

Listen and feel the word of God over you. Take notes on what you felt as the word of God washed over you.

_____
_____
_____
_____
_____
_____

Second Reading

Bring awareness and mindfulness to anything the Lord is pointing out and offer them to God. Take notes on anything that is highlighted.

_____
_____
_____
_____
_____
_____

Third Reading

Ask God about the highlighted things. Do you feel called to do anything? Listen to God and take notes on anything you hear.

_____
_____
_____
_____
_____
_____

Date _____

Psalm 23
23:1-4

Use QR code to access the listening prayer videos

Yahweh is my shepherd: I shall lack nothing. He makes me lie down in green pastures. He leads me beside still waters. He restores my soul. He guides me in the paths of righteousness for his name's sake. Even though I walk through the valley of the shadow of death, I will fear no evil, for you are with me.

Daily Gratitude

I am grateful for...

1 _____

2 _____

3 _____

Today would be great if...

1 _____

2 _____

What affirmations does God have for you today?

1 _____

2 _____

Who would you like to pray for and bless today?

1 _____

2 _____

Listening Prayer

Read or listen to the scripture, follow the prompts in silence for 1-2 min.

First Reading

Listen and feel the word of God over you. Take notes on what you felt as the word of God washed over you.

_____
_____
_____
_____
_____
_____

Second Reading

Bring awareness and mindfulness to anything the Lord is pointing out and offer them to God. Take notes on anything that is highlighted.

_____
_____
_____
_____
_____
_____

Third Reading

Ask God about the highlighted things. Do you feel called to do anything? Listen to God and take notes on anything you hear.

_____
_____
_____
_____
_____
_____

Date

Psalm 24
24:7-10

Use QR code to access the listening prayer videos

Lift up your heads, you gates! Be lifted up, you everlasting doors, and the King of glory will come in. Who is the King of glory? Yahweh strong and mighty, Yahweh mighty in battle. Lift up your heads, you gates; yes, lift them up, you everlasting doors, and the King of glory will come in. Who is this King of glory? Yahweh of Armies is the King of glory! Selah.

Daily Gratitude

I am grateful for...

1
2
3

Today would be great if...

1
2

What affirmations does God have for you today?

1
2

Who would you like to pray for and bless today?

1
2

Listening Prayer

Read or listen to the scripture, follow the prompts in silence for 1-2 min.

First Reading

Listen and feel the word of God over you. Take notes on what you felt as the word of God washed over you.

_____
_____
_____
_____
_____

Second Reading

Bring awareness and mindfulness to anything the Lord is pointing out and offer them to God. Take notes on anything that is highlighted.

_____
_____
_____
_____
_____

Third Reading

Ask God about the highlighted things. Do you feel called to do anything? Listen to God and take notes on anything you hear.

_____
_____
_____
_____
_____
_____

Date _____

Psalm 25
25:12-14

Use QR code to access the listening prayer videos

WHAT MAN IS HE WHO FEARS YAHWEH? HE SHALL INSTRUCT HIM IN THE WAY THAT HE SHALL CHOOSE. HIS SOUL WILL DWELL AT EASE. HIS OFFSPRING WILL INHERIT THE LAND. THE FRIENDSHIP OF YAHWEH IS WITH THOSE WHO FEAR HIM. HE WILL SHOW THEM HIS COVENANT.

Daily Gratitude

I am grateful for...

1 _____
2 _____
3 _____

Today would be great if...

1 _____
2 _____

What affirmations does God have for you today?

1 _____
2 _____

Who would you like to pray for and bless today?

1 _____
2 _____

Listening Prayer

Read or listen to the scripture, follow the prompts in silence for 1-2 min.

First Reading

Listen and feel the word of God over you. Take notes on what you felt as the word of God washed over you.

Second Reading

Bring awareness and mindfulness to anything the Lord is pointing out and offer them to God. Take notes on anything that is highlighted.

Third Reading

Ask God about the highlighted things. Do you feel called to do anything? Listen to God and take notes on anything you hear.

Date: _____

Psalm 26
26:2-5

Use QR code to access the listening prayer videos

Examine me, Yahweh, and prove me. Try my heart and my mind. For your loving kindness is before my eyes. I have walked in your truth. I have not sat with deceitful men, neither will I go in with hypocrites. I hate the assembly of evildoers, and will not sit with the wicked.

Daily Gratitude

I am grateful for...

1. _____
2. _____
3. _____

Today would be great if...

1. _____
2. _____

What affirmations does God have for you today?

1. _____
2. _____

Who would you like to pray for and bless today?

1. _____
2. _____

Listening Prayer

Read or listen to the scripture, follow the prompts in silence for 1-2 min.

First Reading

Listen and feel the word of God over you. Take notes on what you felt as the word of God washed over you.

Second Reading

Bring awareness and mindfulness to anything the Lord is pointing out and offer them to God. Take notes on anything that is highlighted.

Third Reading

Ask God about the highlighted things. Do you feel called to do anything? Listen to God and take notes on anything you hear.

Date _____

Psalm 27
27:1

Use QR code to access the listening prayer videos

YAHWEH IS MY LIGHT AND MY SALVATION. WHOM SHALL I FEAR? YAHWEH IS THE STRENGTH OF MY LIFE. OF WHOM SHALL I BE AFRAID?

Daily Gratitude

I am grateful for...

1 _____
2 _____
3 _____

Today would be great if...

1 _____
2 _____

What affirmations does God have for you today?

1 _____
2 _____

Who would you like to pray for and bless today?

1 _____
2 _____

Listening Prayer

Read or listen to the scripture, follow the prompts in silence for 1-2 min.

First Reading

Listen and feel the word of God over you. Take notes on what you felt as the word of God washed over you.

_____
_____
_____
_____
_____
_____

Second Reading

Bring awareness and mindfulness to anything the Lord is pointing out and offer them to God. Take notes on anything that is highlighted.

_____
_____
_____
_____
_____
_____

Third Reading

Ask God about the highlighted things. Do you feel called to do anything? Listen to God and take notes on anything you hear.

_____
_____
_____
_____
_____
_____

Date: _____

Psalm 28
28:6-9

Use QR code to access the listening prayer videos

Blessed be Yahweh, because he has heard the voice of my petitions. Yahweh is my strength and my shield. My heart has trusted in him, and I am helped. Therefore my heart greatly rejoices. With my song I will thank him. Yahweh is their strength. He is a stronghold of salvation to his anointed. Save your people, and bless your inheritance. Be their shepherd also, and bear them up forever.

Daily Gratitude

I am grateful for...

1 _____
2 _____
3 _____

Today would be great if...

1 _____
2 _____

What affirmations does God have for you today?

1 _____
2 _____

Who would you like to pray for and bless today?

1 _____
2 _____

Listening Prayer

Read or listen to the scripture, follow the prompts in silence for 1-2 min.

First Reading

Listen and feel the word of God over you. Take notes on what you felt as the word of God washed over you.

___
___
___
___
___
___

Second Reading

Bring awareness and mindfulness to anything the Lord is pointing out and offer them to God. Take notes on anything that is highlighted.

___
___
___
___
___
___

Third Reading

Ask God about the highlighted things. Do you feel called to do anything? Listen to God and take notes on anything you hear.

___
___
___
___
___
___

Date

Psalm 29
29:1-2 & 10-11

Ascribe to Yahweh, you sons of the mighty, ascribe to Yahweh glory and strength. Ascribe to Yahweh the glory due to his name. Worship Yahweh in holy array... Yahweh sat enthroned at the Flood. Yes, Yahweh sits as King forever. Yahweh will give strength to his people. Yahweh will bless his people with peace.

Daily Gratitude

I am grateful for...

1
2
3

Today would be great if...

1
2

What affirmations does God have for you today?

1
2

Who would you like to pray for and bless today?

1
2

Listening Prayer

Read or listen to the scripture, follow the prompts in silence for 1-2 min.

First Reading

Listen and feel the word of God over you. Take notes on what you felt as the word of God washed over you.

_____
_____
_____
_____
_____
_____

Second Reading

Bring awareness and mindfulness to anything the Lord is pointing out and offer them to God. Take notes on anything that is highlighted.

_____
_____
_____
_____
_____
_____

Third Reading

Ask God about the highlighted things. Do you feel called to do anything? Listen to God and take notes on anything you hear.

_____
_____
_____
_____
_____
_____

Date _____

Psalm 30
30:11-12

Use QR code to access the listening prayer videos

You have turned my mourning into dancing for me. You have removed my sackcloth, and clothed me with gladness, to the end that my heart may sing praise to you, and not be silent. Yahweh my God, I will give thanks to you forever!

Daily Gratitude

I am grateful for...

1 _____

2 _____

3 _____

Today would be great if...

1 _____

2 _____

What affirmations does God have for you today?

1 _____

2 _____

Who would you like to pray for and bless today?

1 _____

2 _____

Listening Prayer

Read or listen to the scripture, follow the prompts in silence for 1-2 min.

First Reading

Listen and feel the word of God over you. Take notes on what you felt as the word of God washed over you.

_____
_____
_____
_____
_____
_____

Second Reading

Bring awareness and mindfulness to anything the Lord is pointing out and offer them to God. Take notes on anything that is highlighted.

_____
_____
_____
_____
_____

Third Reading

Ask God about the highlighted things. Do you feel called to do anything? Listen to God and take notes on anything you hear.

_____
_____
_____
_____
_____
_____

Date _____

Psalm 31
31:21-24

Use QR code to access the listening prayer videos

Praise be to Yahweh, for he has shown me his marvelous loving kindness in a strong city. As for me, I said in my haste, "I am cut off from before your eyes." Nevertheless you heard the voice of my petitions when I cried to you. Oh love Yahweh, all you his saints! Yahweh preserves the faithful, and fully recompenses him who behaves arrogantly. Be strong, and let your heart take courage.

Daily Gratitude

I am grateful for...

1 _____

2 _____

3 _____

Today would be great if...

1 _____

2 _____

What affirmations does God have for you today?

1 _____

2 _____

Who would you like to pray for and bless today?

1 _____

2 _____

Listening Prayer

Read or listen to the scripture, follow the prompts in silence for 1-2 min.

First Reading

Listen and feel the word of God over you. Take notes on what you felt as the word of God washed over you.

_____
_____
_____
_____
_____
_____

Second Reading

Bring awareness and mindfulness to anything the Lord is pointing out and offer them to God. Take notes on anything that is highlighted.

_____
_____
_____
_____
_____
_____

Third Reading

Ask God about the highlighted things. Do you feel called to do anything? Listen to God and take notes on anything you hear.

_____
_____
_____
_____
_____
_____

Date _____

Psalm 32
32:1-3 & 5

Use QR code to access the listening prayer videos

Blessed is he whose disobedience is forgiven, whose sin is covered. Blessed is the man to whom Yahweh doesn't impute iniquity, in whose spirit there is no deceit. When I kept silence, my bones wasted away through my groaning all day long… I said, I will confess my transgressions to Yahweh, and you forgave the iniquity of my sin. Selah.

Daily Gratitude

I am grateful for...

1 _____
2 _____
3 _____

Today would be great if...

1 _____
2 _____

What affirmations does God have for you today?

1 _____
2 _____

Who would you like to pray for and bless today?

1 _____
2 _____

Listening Prayer

Read or listen to the scripture, follow the prompts in silence for 1-2 min.

First Reading

Listen and feel the word of God over you. Take notes on what you felt as the word of God washed over you.

_____
_____
_____
_____
_____
_____

Second Reading

Bring awareness and mindfulness to anything the Lord is pointing out and offer them to God. Take notes on anything that is highlighted.

_____
_____
_____
_____
_____
_____

Third Reading

Ask God about the highlighted things. Do you feel called to do anything? Listen to God and take notes on anything you hear.

_____
_____
_____
_____
_____
_____

Date _____

Psalm 33
33:1-5

Rejoice in Yahweh, you righteous! Praise is fitting for the upright. Give thanks to Yahweh with the lyre. Sing praises to him with the harp of ten strings. Sing to him a new song. Play skillfully with a shout of joy! For Yahweh's word is right. All his work is done in faithfulness. He loves righteousness and justice. The earth is full of the loving kindness of Yahweh.

Daily Gratitude

I am grateful for...

1 _____

2 _____

3 _____

Today would be great if...

1 _____

2 _____

What affirmations does God have for you today?

1 _____

2 _____

Who would you like to pray for and bless today?

1 _____

2 _____

Listening Prayer

Read or listen to the scripture, follow the prompts in silence for 1-2 min.

First Reading

Listen and feel the word of God over you. Take notes on what you felt as the word of God washed over you.

_____
_____
_____
_____
_____
_____

Second Reading

Bring awareness and mindfulness to anything the Lord is pointing out and offer them to God. Take notes on anything that is highlighted.

_____
_____
_____
_____
_____
_____

Third Reading

Ask God about the highlighted things. Do you feel called to do anything? Listen to God and take notes on anything you hear.

_____
_____
_____
_____
_____
_____

Date _____

Psalm 34
34:7-10

Use QR code to access the listening prayer videos

Yahweh's angel encamps around those who fear him, and delivers them. Oh taste and see that Yahweh is good. Blessed is the man who takes refuge in him. Oh fear Yahweh, you his saints, for there is no lack with those who fear him. The young lions do lack, and suffer hunger, but those who seek Yahweh shall not lack any good thing.

Daily Gratitude

I am grateful for...

1 _____

2 _____

3 _____

Today would be great if...

1 _____

2 _____

What affirmations does God have for you today?

1 _____

2 _____

Who would you like to pray for and bless today?

1 _____

2 _____

Listening Prayer

Read or listen to the scripture, follow the prompts in silence for 1-2 min.

First Reading

Listen and feel the word of God over you. Take notes on what you felt as the word of God washed over you.

_____
_____
_____
_____
_____
_____

Second Reading

Bring awareness and mindfulness to anything the Lord is pointing out and offer them to God. Take notes on anything that is highlighted.

_____
_____
_____
_____
_____

Third Reading

Ask God about the highlighted things. Do you feel called to do anything? Listen to God and take notes on anything you hear.

_____
_____
_____
_____
_____
_____

Date

Psalm 35
35:27-28

Use QR code to access the listening prayer videos

Let those who favor my righteous cause shout for joy and be glad. Yes, let them say continually, "May Yahweh be magnified, who has pleasure in the prosperity of his servant!" My tongue shall talk about your righteousness and about your praise all day long.

Daily Gratitude

I am grateful for...

1
2
3

Today would be great if...

1
2

What affirmations does God have for you today?

1
2

Who would you like to pray for and bless today?

1
2

Listening Prayer

Read or listen to the scripture, follow the prompts in silence for 1-2 min.

First Reading

Listen and feel the word of God over you. Take notes on what you felt as the word of God washed over you.

_____
_____
_____
_____
_____
_____

Second Reading

Bring awareness and mindfulness to anything the Lord is pointing out and offer them to God. Take notes on anything that is highlighted.

_____
_____
_____
_____
_____
_____

Third Reading

Ask God about the highlighted things. Do you feel called to do anything? Listen to God and take notes on anything you hear.

_____
_____
_____
_____
_____
_____

Date

Psalm 36
36:7-10

Use QR code to access the listening prayer videos

THE CHILDREN OF MEN TAKE REFUGE UNDER THE SHADOW OF YOUR WINGS. THEY SHALL BE ABUNDANTLY SATISFIED WITH THE ABUNDANCE OF YOUR HOUSE. YOU WILL MAKE THEM DRINK OF THE RIVER OF YOUR PLEASURES. FOR WITH YOU IS THE SPRING OF LIFE. IN YOUR LIGHT WE WILL SEE LIGHT. OH CONTINUE YOUR LOVING KINDNESS TO THOSE WHO KNOW YOU, YOUR RIGHTEOUSNESS TO THE UPRIGHT IN HEART.

Daily Gratitude

I am grateful for...

1

2

3

Today would be great if...

1

2

What affirmations does God have for you today?

1

2

Who would you like to pray for and bless today?

1

2

Listening Prayer

Read or listen to the scripture, follow the prompts in silence for 1-2 min.

First Reading

Listen and feel the word of God over you. Take notes on what you felt as the word of God washed over you.

_____
_____
_____
_____
_____
_____

Second Reading

Bring awareness and mindfulness to anything the Lord is pointing out and offer them to God. Take notes on anything that is highlighted.

_____
_____
_____
_____
_____
_____

Third Reading

Ask God about the highlighted things. Do you feel called to do anything? Listen to God and take notes on anything you hear.

_____
_____
_____
_____
_____
_____

Date

Psalm 37
37:39-40

Use QR code to access the listening prayer videos

BUT THE SALVATION OF THE RIGHTEOUS IS FROM YAHWEH. HE IS THEIR STRONGHOLD IN THE TIME OF TROUBLE. YAHWEH HELPS THEM AND RESCUES THEM. HE RESCUES THEM FROM THE WICKED AND SAVES THEM BECAUSE THEY HAVE TAKEN REFUGE IN HIM.

Daily Gratitude

I am grateful for...

1
2
3

Today would be great if...

1
2

What affirmations does God have for you today?

1
2

Who would you like to pray for and bless today?

1
2

Listening Prayer

Read or listen to the scripture, follow the prompts in silence for 1-2 min.

First Reading

Listen and feel the word of God over you. Take notes on what you felt as the word of God washed over you.

_____
_____
_____
_____
_____
_____

Second Reading

Bring awareness and mindfulness to anything the Lord is pointing out and offer them to God. Take notes on anything that is highlighted.

_____
_____
_____
_____
_____
_____

Third Reading

Ask God about the highlighted things. Do you feel called to do anything? Listen to God and take notes on anything you hear.

_____
_____
_____
_____
_____
_____

Date

Psalm 38
38:15-18 & 21-22

Use QR code to access the listening prayer videos

For I hope in you, Yahweh. You will answer, Lord my God. For I said, "Don't let them gloat over me, or exalt themselves over me when my foot slips." For I am ready to fall. My pain is continually before me. For I will declare my iniquity. I will be sorry for my sin... Don't forsake me, Yahweh. My God, don't be far from me. Hurry to help me, Lord, my salvation.

Daily Gratitude

I am grateful for...

1
2
3

Today would be great if...

1
2

What affirmations does God have for you today?

1
2

Who would you like to pray for and bless today?

1
2

Listening Prayer

Read or listen to the scripture, follow the prompts in silence for 1-2 min.

First Reading

Listen and feel the word of God over you. Take notes on what you felt as the word of God washed over you.

_____
_____
_____
_____
_____
_____

Second Reading

Bring awareness and mindfulness to anything the Lord is pointing out and offer them to God. Take notes on anything that is highlighted.

_____
_____
_____
_____
_____
_____

Third Reading

Ask God about the highlighted things. Do you feel called to do anything? Listen to God and take notes on anything you hear.

_____
_____
_____
_____
_____
_____

Date

Psalm 39
39:7-9

Use QR code to access the listening prayer videos

> Now, Lord, what do I wait for? My hope is in you. Deliver me from all my transgressions. Don't make me the reproach of the foolish. I was mute. I didn't open my mouth, because you did it.

Daily Gratitude

I am grateful for...

1. _____
2. _____
3. _____

Today would be great if...

1. _____
2. _____

What affirmations does God have for you today?

1. _____
2. _____

Who would you like to pray for and bless today?

1. _____
2. _____

Listening Prayer

Read or listen to the scripture, follow the prompts in silence for 1-2 min.

First Reading

Listen and feel the word of God over you. Take notes on what you felt as the word of God washed over you.

_____
_____
_____
_____
_____
_____

Second Reading

Bring awareness and mindfulness to anything the Lord is pointing out and offer them to God. Take notes on anything that is highlighted.

_____
_____
_____
_____
_____
_____

Third Reading

Ask God about the highlighted things. Do you feel called to do anything? Listen to God and take notes on anything you hear.

_____
_____
_____
_____
_____
_____

Date

Psalm 40
40:1-3

Use QR code to access the listening prayer videos

I WAITED PATIENTLY FOR YAHWEH. HE TURNED TO ME, AND HEARD MY CRY. HE BROUGHT ME UP ALSO OUT OF A HORRIBLE PIT, OUT OF THE MIRY CLAY. HE SET MY FEET ON A ROCK, AND GAVE ME A FIRM PLACE TO STAND. HE HAS PUT A NEW SONG IN MY MOUTH, EVEN PRAISE TO OUR GOD. MANY SHALL SEE IT, AND FEAR, AND SHALL TRUST IN YAHWEH.

Daily Gratitude

I am grateful for...

1
2
3

Today would be great if...

1
2

What affirmations does God have for you today?

1
2

Who would you like to pray for and bless today?

1
2

Listening Prayer

Read or listen to the scripture, follow the prompts in silence for 1-2 min.

First Reading

Listen and feel the word of God over you. Take notes on what you felt as the word of God washed over you.

_____
_____
_____
_____
_____
_____

Second Reading

Bring awareness and mindfulness to anything the Lord is pointing out and offer them to God. Take notes on anything that is highlighted.

_____
_____
_____
_____
_____
_____

Third Reading

Ask God about the highlighted things. Do you feel called to do anything? Listen to God and take notes on anything you hear.

_____
_____
_____
_____
_____
_____

Date: _____

Psalm 41
41:1-2

Use QR code to access the listening prayer videos

BLESSED IS HE WHO CONSIDERS THE POOR. YAHWEH WILL DELIVER HIM IN THE DAY OF EVIL. YAHWEH WILL PRESERVE HIM, AND KEEP HIM ALIVE. HE SHALL BE BLESSED ON THE EARTH, AND HE WILL NOT SURRENDER HIM TO THE WILL OF HIS ENEMIES.

Daily Gratitude

I am grateful for...

1. _____
2. _____
3. _____

Today would be great if...

1. _____
2. _____

What affirmations does God have for you today?

1. _____
2. _____

Who would you like to pray for and bless today?

1. _____
2. _____

Listening Prayer

Read or listen to the scripture, follow the prompts in silence for 1-2 min.

First Reading

Listen and feel the word of God over you. Take notes on what you felt as the word of God washed over you.

_____

_____

_____

_____

_____

Second Reading

Bring awareness and mindfulness to anything the Lord is pointing out and offer them to God. Take notes on anything that is highlighted.

_____

_____

_____

_____

_____

Third Reading

Ask God about the highlighted things. Do you feel called to do anything? Listen to God and take notes on anything you hear.

_____

_____

_____

_____

_____

Date _____

Use QR code to access the listening prayer videos

Psalm 42
42:6-7

MY GOD, MY SOUL IS IN DESPAIR WITHIN ME. THEREFORE I REMEMBER YOU FROM THE LAND OF THE JORDAN, THE HEIGHTS OF HERMON, FROM THE HILL MIZAR. DEEP CALLS TO DEEP AT THE NOISE OF YOUR WATERFALLS. ALL YOUR WAVES AND YOUR BILLOWS HAVE SWEPT OVER ME.

Daily Gratitude

I am grateful for...

1 _____

2 _____

3 _____

Today would be great if...

1 _____

2 _____

What affirmations does God have for you today?

1 _____

2 _____

Who would you like to pray for and bless today?

1 _____

2 _____

Listening Prayer

Read or listen to the scripture, follow the prompts in silence for 1-2 min.

First Reading

Listen and feel the word of God over you. Take notes on what you felt as the word of God washed over you.

_____
_____
_____
_____
_____
_____

Second Reading

Bring awareness and mindfulness to anything the Lord is pointing out and offer them to God. Take notes on anything that is highlighted.

_____
_____
_____
_____
_____
_____

Third Reading

Ask God about the highlighted things. Do you feel called to do anything? Listen to God and take notes on anything you hear.

_____
_____
_____
_____
_____
_____

Date _____

Psalm 43
43:2-4

Use QR code to access the listening prayer videos

For you are the God of my strength. Why have you rejected me? Why do I go mourning because of the oppression of the enemy? Oh, send out your light and your truth. Let them lead me. Let them bring me to your holy hill, to your tents. Then I will go to the altar of God, to God, my exceeding joy. I will praise you on the harp, God, my God.

Daily Gratitude

I am grateful for...

1 _____
2 _____
3 _____

Today would be great if...

1 _____
2 _____

What affirmations does God have for you today?

1 _____
2 _____

Who would you like to pray for and bless today?

1 _____
2 _____

Listening Prayer

Read or listen to the scripture, follow the prompts in silence for 1-2 min.

First Reading

Listen and feel the word of God over you. Take notes on what you felt as the word of God washed over you.

_____
_____
_____
_____
_____
_____

Second Reading

Bring awareness and mindfulness to anything the Lord is pointing out and offer them to God. Take notes on anything that is highlighted.

_____
_____
_____
_____
_____

Third Reading

Ask God about the highlighted things. Do you feel called to do anything? Listen to God and take notes on anything you hear.

_____
_____
_____
_____
_____
_____

Date

Psalm 44
44:23-26

Use QR code to access the listening prayer videos

WAKE UP! WHY DO YOU SLEEP, LORD? ARISE! DON'T REJECT US FOREVER. WHY DO YOU HIDE YOUR FACE, AND FORGET OUR AFFLICTION AND OUR OPPRESSION? FOR OUR SOUL IS BOWED DOWN TO THE DUST. OUR BODY CLINGS TO THE EARTH. RISE UP TO HELP US. REDEEM US FOR YOUR LOVING KINDNESS' SAKE.

Daily Gratitude

I am grateful for...

1
2
3

Today would be great if...

1
2

What affirmations does God have for you today?

1
2

Who would you like to pray for and bless today?

1
2

Listening Prayer

Read or listen to the scripture, follow the prompts in silence for 1-2 min.

First Reading

Listen and feel the word of God over you. Take notes on what you felt as the word of God washed over you.

_____
_____
_____
_____
_____

Second Reading

Bring awareness and mindfulness to anything the Lord is pointing out and offer them to God. Take notes on anything that is highlighted.

_____
_____
_____
_____
_____

Third Reading

Ask God about the highlighted things. Do you feel called to do anything? Listen to God and take notes on anything you hear.

_____
_____
_____
_____
_____

Date _____

Psalm 45
45:6-7

Use QR code to access the listening prayer videos

YOUR THRONE, GOD, IS FOREVER AND EVER. A SCEPTER OF EQUITY IS THE SCEPTER OF YOUR KINGDOM. YOU HAVE LOVED RIGHTEOUSNESS, AND HATED WICKEDNESS. THEREFORE GOD, YOUR GOD, HAS ANOINTED YOU WITH THE OIL OF GLADNESS ABOVE YOUR FELLOWS.

Daily Gratitude

I am grateful for...

1 _____
2 _____
3 _____

Today would be great if...

1 _____
2 _____

What affirmations does God have for you today?

1 _____
2 _____

Who would you like to pray for and bless today?

1 _____
2 _____

Listening Prayer

Read or listen to the scripture, follow the prompts in silence for 1-2 min.

First Reading

Listen and feel the word of God over you. Take notes on what you felt as the word of God washed over you.

_____
_____
_____
_____
_____
_____

Second Reading

Bring awareness and mindfulness to anything the Lord is pointing out and offer them to God. Take notes on anything that is highlighted.

_____
_____
_____
_____
_____
_____

Third Reading

Ask God about the highlighted things. Do you feel called to do anything? Listen to God and take notes on anything you hear.

_____
_____
_____
_____
_____
_____

Date _____

Psalm 46
46:10-11

Use QR code to access the listening prayer videos

"BE STILL, AND KNOW THAT I AM GOD. I WILL BE EXALTED AMONG THE NATIONS. I WILL BE EXALTED IN THE EARTH." YAHWEH OF ARMIES IS WITH US. THE GOD OF JACOB IS OUR REFUGE. SELAH.

Daily Gratitude

I am grateful for...

1 _____
2 _____
3 _____

Today would be great if...

1 _____
2 _____

What affirmations does God have for you today?

1 _____
2 _____

Who would you like to pray for and bless today?

1 _____
2 _____

Listening Prayer

Read or listen to the scripture, follow the prompts in silence for 1-2 min.

First Reading

Listen and feel the word of God over you. Take notes on what you felt as the word of God washed over you.

Second Reading

Bring awareness and mindfulness to anything the Lord is pointing out and offer them to God. Take notes on anything that is highlighted.

Third Reading

Ask God about the highlighted things. Do you feel called to do anything? Listen to God and take notes on anything you hear.

Date

Psalm 47
47:1-4

Use QR code to access the listening prayer videos

OH CLAP YOUR HANDS, ALL YOU NATIONS. SHOUT TO GOD WITH THE VOICE OF TRIUMPH! FOR YAHWEH MOST HIGH IS AWESOME. HE IS A GREAT KING OVER ALL THE EARTH. HE SUBDUES NATIONS UNDER US, AND PEOPLES UNDER OUR FEET. HE CHOOSES OUR INHERITANCE FOR US, THE GLORY OF JACOB WHOM HE LOVED. SELAH.

Daily Gratitude

I am grateful for...

1
2
3

Today would be great if...

1
2

What affirmations does God have for you today?

1
2

Who would you like to pray for and bless today?

1
2

Listening Prayer

Read or listen to the scripture, follow the prompts in silence for 1-2 min.

First Reading

Listen and feel the word of God over you. Take notes on what you felt as the word of God washed over you.

_____
_____
_____
_____
_____
_____

Second Reading

Bring awareness and mindfulness to anything the Lord is pointing out and offer them to God. Take notes on anything that is highlighted.

_____
_____
_____
_____
_____
_____

Third Reading

Ask God about the highlighted things. Do you feel called to do anything? Listen to God and take notes on anything you hear.

_____
_____
_____
_____
_____
_____

Date

Psalm 48
48:8-11

Use QR code to access the listening prayer videos

AS WE HAVE HEARD, SO WE HAVE SEEN, IN THE CITY OF YAHWEH OF ARMIES, IN THE CITY OF OUR GOD. GOD WILL ESTABLISH IT FOREVER. SELAH. WE HAVE THOUGHT ABOUT YOUR LOVING KINDNESS, GOD, IN THE MIDDLE OF YOUR TEMPLE. AS IS YOUR NAME, GOD, SO IS YOUR PRAISE TO THE ENDS OF THE EARTH. YOUR RIGHT HAND IS FULL OF RIGHTEOUSNESS. LET MOUNT ZION BE GLAD! LET THE DAUGHTERS OF JUDAH REJOICE BECAUSE OF YOUR JUDGMENTS.

Daily Gratitude

I am grateful for...

1
2
3

Today would be great if...

1
2

What affirmations does God have for you today?

1
2

Who would you like to pray for and bless today?

1
2

Listening Prayer

Read or listen to the scripture, follow the prompts in silence for 1-2 min.

First Reading

Listen and feel the word of God over you. Take notes on what you felt as the word of God washed over you.

_____
_____
_____
_____
_____
_____

Second Reading

Bring awareness and mindfulness to anything the Lord is pointing out and offer them to God. Take notes on anything that is highlighted.

_____
_____
_____
_____
_____
_____

Third Reading

Ask God about the highlighted things. Do you feel called to do anything? Listen to God and take notes on anything you hear.

_____
_____
_____
_____
_____
_____

Date

Psalm 49
49:10-12

Use QR code to access the listening prayer videos

For he sees that wise men die; likewise the fool and the senseless perish, and leave their wealth to others. Their inward thought is that their houses will endure forever, and their dwelling places to all generations. They name their lands after themselves. But man, despite his riches, doesn't endure. He is like the animals that perish.

Daily Gratitude

I am grateful for...

1
2
3

Today would be great if...

1
2

What affirmations does God have for you today?

1
2

Who would you like to pray for and bless today?

1
2

Listening Prayer

Read or listen to the scripture, follow the prompts in silence for 1-2 min.

First Reading

Listen and feel the word of God over you. Take notes on what you felt as the word of God washed over you.

_____
_____
_____
_____
_____
_____
_____

Second Reading

Bring awareness and mindfulness to anything the Lord is pointing out and offer them to God. Take notes on anything that is highlighted.

_____
_____
_____
_____
_____
_____
_____

Third Reading

Ask God about the highlighted things. Do you feel called to do anything? Listen to God and take notes on anything you hear.

_____
_____
_____
_____
_____
_____
_____

Date: _____

Psalm 50

Use QR code to access the listening prayer videos

50:8-10 & 14-15

"I don't rebuke you for your sacrifices. Your burnt offerings are continually before me. I have no need for a bull from your stall, nor male goats from your pens. For every animal of the forest is mine, and the livestock on a thousand hills. Offer to God the sacrifice of thanksgiving. Pay your vows to the Most High. Call on me in the day of trouble. I will deliver you, and you will honor me."

Daily Gratitude

I am grateful for...

1. _____
2. _____
3. _____

Today would be great if...

1. _____
2. _____

What affirmations does God have for you today?

1. _____
2. _____

Who would you like to pray for and bless today?

1. _____
2. _____

Listening Prayer

Read or listen to the scripture, follow the prompts in silence for 1-2 min.

First Reading

Listen and feel the word of God over you. Take notes on what you felt as the word of God washed over you.

_____
_____
_____
_____
_____
_____

Second Reading

Bring awareness and mindfulness to anything the Lord is pointing out and offer them to God. Take notes on anything that is highlighted.

_____
_____
_____
_____
_____

Third Reading

Ask God about the highlighted things. Do you feel called to do anything? Listen to God and take notes on anything you hear.

_____
_____
_____
_____
_____

Want free content?
Sign up at
23streams.com/bonus
Your code: 9j&37C

Follow on:
Youtube

Facebook
Instagram
Tiktok

Please Leave A Review On Amazon

And

Order Your Journal For Psalms 51-100

Shop our other books at 23streams.com

© 23streams. All rights reserved. No part of this publication may be reproduced, distributed, or transmitted, in any form or by any means, including photocopying, recording, or other electronic or mechanical methods, without prior written permission of the publisher, except in the case of brief quotations embodied in critical reviews and certain other noncommercial uses permitted by copyright law.